CW00369807

NARROW GAUGE INTO THE EIGHTIES

G T Heavyside

DAVID & CHARLES

Newton Abbot   London   North Pomfret (Vt)

Heavyside, G T
 Narrow gauge into the eighties.
 1. Railways, Narrow-gauge - Great Britain -
 Pictorial works
 I. Title
 385'.5'0941   HE3816

 ISBN 0-7153-7979-8

© G T Heavyside 1980

All rights reserved. No part of this publication
 may be reproduced, stored in a retrieval
system, or transmitted, in any form or by any
means, electronic, mechanical, photocopying,
recording or otherwise, without the prior
permission of David & Charles (Publishers)
Limited

Typeset by Photoprint, Paignton and
Printed in Great Britain
by Biddles Ltd, Guildford, Surrey
for David & Charles (Publishers) Limited
Brunel House   Newton Abbot   Devon

Published in the United States of America
by David & Charles Inc
North Pomfret   Vermont 05053   USA

Acknowledgements

A goodly number of people have rendered assistance towards completion of this book, some of whom provided facilities for photography, and to all I offer my sincere thanks.

I am also grateful to those who forwarded photographs and the publication of some of these has enabled a much more complete picture of the narrow gauge scene to be documented than would have otherwise been the case. Photographs used have been acknowledged individually.

My special thanks are again due to Chris Makin and Mavis Phillips for their work on the prints and Marlene McPherson for her work at the typewriter.

Bolton, Lancs
January 1980

G T Heavyside

Contents

Introduction

Since the pioneering days of steam railways in Britain when the Stephenson gauge of 4ft 8½in was adopted as standard for the main system, any line with a smaller width between the rails has been classed as narrow gauge. While some of the early mineral waggonways would today be categorised as narrow, and the first railway to use steam locomotives regularly, the rack-rail Middleton Colliery Railway at Leeds in 1812, used a gauge of 4ft 1in, there was little general development of the smaller gauges until the latter part of the nineteenth century.

Once a standard for the gauge was agreed it was obviously desirable, in the best interests of the nation, that the bulk of the railway network should be laid to this measurement, and, in the cause of uniformity, even the highly individualistic Great Western eventually had to bow to the other main companies and replace its broad gauge track with that of standard width.

However there are circumstances where a narrow gauge line offers distinct advantages over its wider gauge counterparts. First they are cheaper to construct and maintain since less land is required for the permanent way, and second with tighter curves possible expensive earthworks can often be avoided. Thus in mountainous and thinly populated areas, where potential traffic would not support the higher overheads of a standard or broad gauge line, they could sometimes be the only viable means of providing rail access. In these situations the need to change mode of travel at a railhead, and the slow speeds usually appertaining, are of secondary importance.

In addition to the desire for a recognised standard the early growth of the narrow gauge was also retarded because steam was not harnessed to the smaller lines until 1863 (34 years after the Rainhill trials), when the 1ft 11½in gauge Festiniog Railway in North Wales, originally built as a narrow gauge waggonway in 1836, took delivery of its first two locomotives. These were two 0-4-0Ts with tenders, *Princess* and *Prince* built by George England & Co Ltd of London, the engines, rebuilt as 0-4-0STs with tenders, still being on the Festiniog's books. At the time of delivery the Festiniog was solely a slate carrying line but two years later it introduced a passenger service, again the first over such narrow track.

From then on, the output of narrow gauge steam engines from the factories of British locomotive builders gradually increased as they sought to satisfy the demands of those wishing to use a small gauge, although a considerable percentage went overseas, often to countries where the main systems were built to narrow proportions, as in South Africa where the 3ft 6in gauge holds sway.

However despite the availability of the iron horse, apart from Ireland where a sizeable mileage of 3ft wide track was put down, only a small number of public narrow gauge railways were built in the British Isles, these mainly emerging during the latter part of the Victorian era. Maybe this is not surprising in view of the rapid expansion of the standard and GWR broad gauge systems that ultimately linked almost every town of any importance on the mainland.

Building continued well into the twentieth century, the last of this phase being the 15in gauge Romney Hythe & Dymchurch Railway opened in 1927. In some ways this belies the fact that life for the narrow gauge was far from easy, for by 1950 many lines had closed their doors, some 20 or more years before that, vanquished by the combined forces of a stringent financial climate, the rigours of the two world wars, and growing road competition. In many cases the long term prospects of the few that did survive looked bleak, including those taken

Epitome of much of the narrow gauge steam scene today — a new line using an otherwise redundant locomotive. The engine is 0-4-0WT No 1 *Caledonia* built by Andrew Barclay of Kilmarnock in 1931, works No 995, and is seen here running along the 1971 opened 2ft gauge Hollycombe Woodland Railway, Liphook, Hampshire, on 11 June 1978. The engine was previously employed in Durham and at Port Dinorwic in North Wales. *(G T Heavyside)*

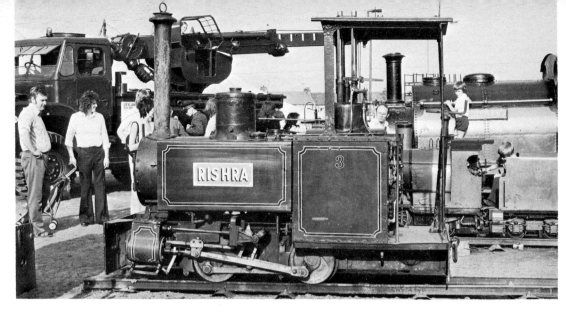

under the wing of British Railways upon nationalisation in 1948.

In Britain it was as industrial lines that the narrow gauge came into its own, economy of construction and its easy ability to negotiate narrow confines making it ideal for development as a means of transport at mines (both above and below ground), quarries, peat bogs, and large factories. Some have taken advantage of the lightweight nature of the track, which can be slewed easily to keep wagon loading points as near as possible to working areas — especially useful at quarries, etc, where faces are continually changing.

In recent times this aspect of operations has also witnessed a general decline and in addition to site closures many have found conveyor belts, dumper trucks, and road haulage more economic and practical, although even so there is still a considerable amount of narrow gauge activity at industrial locations. Unfortunately steam locomotives are no longer evident, having been superseded by the internal combustion engine.

It is against this background that the renaissance of the narrow gauge is set, this epoch dating from October 1950 when a small group of people met in a Birmingham hotel with the avowed intention of finding a solution to keeping open the Talyllyn Railway, then seemingly destined to close, following the owner's death. It is now part of railway folklore how they founded the Talyllyn Railway Preservation Society which subsequently transformed the woebegone state of the Talyllyn into the workmanlike institution it is today, at the same time kindling the flame which sparked the reincarna-

tion of many lines — both standard as well as narrow gauges.

The Talyllyn RPS first steamed trains out of Tywyn during the summer of 1951, and this says much for the vision and courage of those involved, since, in a way never seen before, management and labour were principally vested in volunteers, many of whom had little or no previous railway operating experience. Following their example protagonists of the Festiniog Railway were soon at work, and their efforts resulted in steam once more rumbling across the Cob from Porthmadog in 1955 after an absence of nine years.

At this time a few lines, like the Romney, Hythe & Dymchurch and the rack-rail Snowdon Mountain Railway, functioned on a commercial basis, but at the Festiniog reopening Talyllyn personnel could be forgiven if they cast an anxious glance along the West Wales coast, and later elsewhere, as other railways that relied mainly on voluntary labour were revived. As the preservation movement gathered momentum many have been concerned as to whether or not the supply of gratis labour would be sufficient to continue servicing all the lines depending on this source of manpower, but happily the story for all gauges is one of resounding success.

While not unnaturally some proposed schemes have fallen by the wayside for one reason or another, even the most optimistic of prophets could hardly have foreseen the proliferation of narrow gauge steam lines that will grace the 1980s. Individually they are distinctive in character, but one common factor is that their patrons, with but a few exceptions, are

travelling purely for pleasure, either on holiday or during a day's outing. Their growing popularity can be measured by the steady upward trend of the graphs recording the total number of visitors, some lines now catering for hundreds of thousands of passengers annually.

Many lines, like the Festiniog and Talyllyn railways, now find themselves listed among the most popular tourist attractions and accordingly have had to expand regularly and improve their services to cope with their ever increasing clientele. This has meant not only purchasing additional motive power and coaching stock, and installing extra passing loops, but also providing adequate refreshment facilities, suitably stocked souvenir shops, establishing museums and picnic areas etc, all of which add to the enjoyment of a family day out.

On the busier lines seven days a week running is the norm during the summer season, which for some has meant abandoning the ideal of relying mainly on voluntary labour in favour of a core of permanent staff supplemented by casuals at peak times. During winter months operating staff usually turn their hands to maintenance work, but even so the assistance of volunteers is still welcomed and encouraged, and in some cases they are vital for the well being of the lines.

There are a number of concerns which strictly are not part of the preservation movement since, like the Vale of Rheidol line and Snowdon Mountain Railway, they continue in pretty much the same way that they have done for decades. With some it is difficult to differentiate accurately in this respect, but

Left: At the Rail 150 celebrations held at Shildon in August 1975 to mark the 150th anniversary of the Stockton & Darlington Railway, as well as the galaxy of standard gauge locomotives that assembled there a place was deservedly found for a number of narrow gauge exhibits. In the forefront here is 2ft gauge Baguley 0-4-0T No 3 *Rishra* from the Leighton Buzzard Narrow Gauge Railway. *(M Wood)*

Above: As a tribute to the former locomotive building company, W.G. Bagnall Ltd, Castle Engine Works, Stafford, one of its products, 2ft gauge 0-4-0ST *Isabel*, works No 1491 and purchased by the Cliffe Hill Granite Co, Markfield, Leics, in 1897, stands in Victoria Gardens, Stafford, opposite the BR station. Between 1876 and 1957 Bagnall constructed 1667 steam engines, some 73 per cent being for narrow gauge lines, although a large proportion were for overseas customers. *(G T Heavyside)*

Below: The swansong of industrial narrow gauge steam in Britain was on Bowaters' 2ft 6in gauge railway at Sittingbourne, Kent, a line used to convey employees as well as freight. In October 1969 part of the line was leased for preservation as a going concern to the Locomotive Club of Great Britain, and under its new operators Bagnall 0-6-2T *Triumph* (works No 2511 of 1934) makes light work of a Sittingbourne to Kemsley train on 13 August 1970. The Sittingbourne & Kemsley Railway as it is known, is now run separately from the LCGB. *(D A Idle)*

Out of little acorns do great oak trees grow! The first seeds of the steam preservation movement as we know it today reach fruition, as 1866-built Fletcher Jennings 0-4-0WT No 2 *Dolgoch* prepares to leave Talyllyn Railway Tywyn Wharf station with the official opening train under the auspices of the newly formed Talyllyn Railway Preservation Society on Whit Monday 1951.
(Courtesy Talyllyn Railway)

whatever their pedigree or present constitution, there is little doubt that all have benefited from the general upsurge of interest in steam railways.

As well as revivals the past 20 years has seen a resurgence of entirely new lines, some operating on a commercial basis with paid staff. They can be located at such diverse places as the grounds of stately homes, amusement parks, zoological gardens, and standard gauge railway centres etc, where they often form part of a series of attractions, while the Bala Lake and Lappa Valley railways utilise trackbeds formerly owned by British Railways.

Like the standard gauge there are lines manned and administered solely by volunteers but these generally, while being run in a professional manner, operate only at weekends and Bank holidays. Also to be mentioned are the short lengths of tracks laid on private land not open to the public and used to exercise a number of engines for the owner's benefit, and perhaps a few guests.

Small in stature narrow gauge stock may be, but in every other respect there is no place for half measures. This is especially so on the operating side, which is subject to statutory procedures and inspection, safety regulations being of paramount importance. Vital, too, is proper staff training, whatever their status, if a line is to function efficiently, while maintenance of stock, buildings, and lineside furniture, must receive due attention if the right image is to be projected to the modern day discerning public.

So far little has been said of the iron horse and it may come as a surprise to learn that over 280 narrow gauge engines are extant in the British Isles, although some are confined to museums as static exhibits. The variety of species is evidenced by the fact that they emanate from the works of over 60 builders, including 16 in mainland Europe and two American factories. Some 21 gauges varying from 15in to 4ft 6in are represented, but the difference in width between some is so infinitesimal that engines on occasions operate over track nominally not of the same width.

Some railways are utilising engines which started their careers on the same metals, but for many there has been a growing requirement to increase their stock of power, a need satisfied by obtaining otherwise redundant locomotives (sometimes in a deplorable condition) from both home and overseas sources. Opportunities

for the individual to buy extra engines has often been limited due to gauge (and sometimes loading gauge) restrictions, a problem overcome in some instances by altering the axle width in order to make locomotives compatible with the track, and similarly coaching stock has been re-gauged. In the case of new lines gauge has often been dictated by the available stock.

Throughout the British Isles steam locomotives built along conventional lines have generally been the rule, with tank engines usually preferred to tender types, these being more suitable for bi-directional running without turning at industrial locations and over the relatively short distances of the public lines. Notable departures from tradition include the Samuel Geoghegan designed engines for the Dublin based Guinness Brewery Railway (described on page 92), and about 50 vertical boilered locomotives to numerous gauges by De Winton & Co of Caernarfon built during Victorian times for the rough tracks endemic at the North Wales slate quarries (see page 30).

While few articulated locomotives have found employment in Britain, the narrow gauge was the inspiration for many of these designs,

10

Left: Nameplate of Romney, Hythe & Dymchurch Railway Pacific No 3 *Southern Maid* over the centre driving wheel splasher. A large percentage of narrow gauge engines are personalised by names, although the majority carry straight plates. *(G T Heavyside)*

Right: The 2ft gauge portable Oldberrow Light Railway on view at a local fete at Henley-in-Arden with Bagnall 0-4-0ST No 2088 *Lady Luxborough,* built in 1918, getting up steam. Over the years some engines have become quite nomadic, their comparative light weight allowing relatively easy transport from one line to another. *(R L Patrick)*

their increased power within limited clearances, coupled to greater flexibility on tight curves, making them ideal work horses on small lines which carry heavy traffic. Examples can be viewed at the National Railway Museum, York — the first Beyer Garratt — and on the Festiniog Railway, which for over 100 years has made extensive use of engines to Robert Fairlie's patent.

Construction of new locomotives continues, albeit on a very limited scale compared with the flow which once departed from the factories. The last to be built for overseas was a 2ft 6in gauge 0-4-2ST by Hunslet in 1971 for the Indonesia Forestry Commission, while a few

have since entered service in Britain, the latest being a Fairlie 0-4-4-0T built for the Festiniog Railway in its own Boston Lodge Works in 1979.

The rise of the present generation of narrow gauge railways has been meteoric, the map on page 12 detailing the geographical spread in England and Wales, where most of the activity is concentrated. It will readily be realised that vast amounts of capital are involved and over the years every avenue of finance has had to be explored, from the usual fund raising efforts to obtaining grants from tourist boards and help from Government sponsored manpower assistance schemes. For some, preservation is still

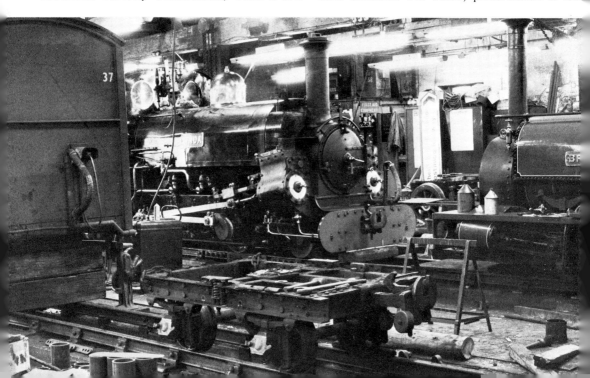

Below left: Many of the railways have well appointed workshops, as at Boston Lodge on the Festiniog Railway, where Hunslet 2-4-0ST plus tender *Linda* and, right, Hunslet 0-4-0ST *Britomart* are seen on 11 September 1978. *(G T Heavyside)*

Below: Builder's plate attached to the latest product from the Festiniog Railway Boston Lodge Works, Fairlie 0-4-4-0T *Iarll Meirionnydd/Earl of Merioneth.*
(G T Heavyside)

their motive, with involvement on a voluntary basis for the sheer joy of working with steam, while others at the opposite end of the spectrum, whose railways are commercial undertakings, depend on the lines for their bread and butter.

The narrow gauge is far from static, one or two new lines currently developing from their present embryo state, while for the management of some lines expansion is the keyword. For all, long term planning is essential and an item to be kept permanently on the agenda.

Narrow track coupled with the iron horse has a charismatic flavour of its own and the following pages depict the current scene in the British Isles, from the main tourist lines to others in the gardens of private houses. The smallest gauge illustrated is 15in, and while some class these as miniature railways I find it difficult to accept lines like the Ravenglass & Eskdale and Romney, Hythe & Dymchurch, which operate intensive services over 7 and 13 miles respectively, in this category. Long ago Sir Arthur P. Heywood decided on 15in as the minimum width acceptable for everyday use and hence the inclusion of this gauge. Equally, though, there are 15in gauge lines serving in the same capacity as the smaller gauge miniatures, effectively as sideshows within a larger attraction, which are not really within the scope of this book.

As we enter the 1980s the smaller versions of Trevithick's invention are still very much a live force and, overall, looking quite healthy. May it be that the narrow gauge will continue to gain strength and give pleasure to many future generations.

12

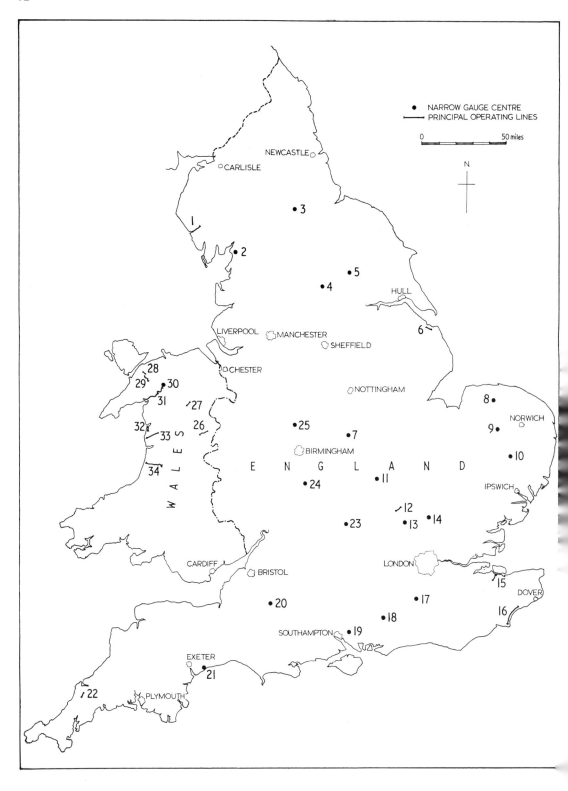

NARROW GAUGE CENTRE
PRINCIPAL OPERATING LINES

0   50 miles

N

NEWCASTLE

CARLISLE

•3

1

•2

•5

•4

HULL

6

LIVERPOOL

MANCHESTER

SHEFFIELD

CHESTER

28

29 •30

31

27

NOTTINGHAM

8•

NORWICH

9•

32

33

26

•25

•7

•10

34

E   N   G   L   A   N   D

•11

IPSWICH

BIRMINGHAM

•24

12

•14

•23

•13

W   A   L   E   S

CARDIFF

BRISTOL

LONDON

15

DOVER

•20

•17

16

•18

SOUTHAMPTON

•19

EXETER

•21

22

PLYMOUTH

Locations featured in England and Wales

Key to Map

England

		Gauge(s)
1	Ravenglass & Eskdale Railway, Ravenglass-Eskdale.	1' 3"
2	Steamtown, Carnforth.	1' 3" *
3	Whorlton Lido, near Barnard Castle.	1' 3"
4	Howdenclough Light Railway, Bruntcliffe, near Leeds.	1' 10¾"
5	National Railway Museum, York.	various *
6	Lincolnshire Coast Light Railway, Humberston-South Sea Lane.	2' 0"
7	Cadeby Light Railway, Cadeby, near Market Bosworth.	2' 0"
8	Thursford Steam Railway, near Fakenham.	1' 10¾"
9	Yaxham Park Light Railway, near East Dereham.	2' 0"
10	Bressingham Steam Museum, Diss.	1' 3" *
		& 60cm
11	Northamptonshire Ironstone Railway Trust, Hunsbury Hill, near Northampton.	metre *
12	Leighton Buzzard Narrow Gauge Railway, Page's Park-Stonehenge.	2' 0"
13	Whipsnade & Umfolozi Railway, Whipsnade Zoo, Dunstable.	2' 6"
		& 3' 6"
14	Knebworth West Park & Wintergreen Railway, Knebworth House, near Stevenage.	1' 11½"
15	Sittingbourne & Kemsley Railway, Sittingbourne-Kemsley Down.	2' 6" *
16	Romney, Hythe & Dymchurch Railway, Hythe-Dungeness.	1' 3"
17	Brockham Museum, Betchworth, near Dorking.	various
18	Hollycombe Woodland Railway, Liphook.	2' 0" *
19	Hampshire Narrow Gauge Railway Society, Durley, near Southampton.	2' 0"
20	Longleat Light Railway, Longleat Park, near Warminster.	1' 3"
21	Bicton Woodland Railway, Bicton Gardens, near Budleigh Salterton.	1' 6"
22	Lappa Valley Railway, Newlyn East, East Wheal Rose Mine-Benny Halt.	1' 3"
23	Blenheim Palace Railway, Woodstock.	1' 3"
24	Oldberrow Light Railway, Henley-in-Arden.	2' 0"
25	Victoria Gardens, Stafford.	2' 0"

Wales

26	Welshpool & Llanfair Railway, Llanfair Caereinion-Sylfaen.	2' 6"
27	Bala Lake Railway, Llanuwchllyn-Bala.	1' 11½"
28	Llanberis Lake Railway, Llanberis Padarn Park-Penllyn.	1' 11½"
29	Snowdon Mountain Railway, Llanberis-Snowdon Summit.	2' 7½"
30	Narrow Gauge Railway Centre, Gloddfa Ganol, Ffestiniog Mountain Tourist Centre, Blaenau Ffestiniog.	various
31	Festiniog Railway, Porthmadog-Tanygrisiau.	1' 11½"
32	Fairbourne Railway, Fairbourne-Barmouth Ferry.	1' 3"
33	Talyllyn Railway, Tywyn-Nant Gwernol.	2' 3"
34	Vale of Rheidol Railway, Aberystwyth-Devil's Bridge.	1' 11½"

Standard gauge engines can also be seen at these locations.

England

England's green and pleasant land, rich in so much, has alas played host to but a few public narrow gauge railways. Ignoring for the moment the 15in gauge, only nine such lines were built during the late nineteenth and early twentieth centuries, and by the start of the second world war in 1939, only the 3ft gauge Rye & Camber Tramway in Sussex still carried passengers. This line was commandeered by the War Department in 1940 but failed to reopen when hostilities ended, while goods traffic on the then one remaining line, the 60cm gauge Ashover Light Railway in Derbyshire, soldiered on until 1950.

Today one can but lament that none of these lines survived long enough to be affected by the subsequent tidal wave of the preservation movement, for such as the Leek & Manifold, with its engines and stock constructed to similar designs to those of the Barsi Light Railway in India, and the 19 mile Lynton & Barnstaple, would surely have been prime candidates for retention, at least in part if not wholly.

It was over the private tracks of industrialists that the majority of England's narrow gauge steam fleet found employment, but those who still favour rail traction now rely on more modern forms of motive power. However two redundant lines from this field have been kept in situ by preservationists, one at Sittingbourne as already pictured on page 7, the other at Leighton Buzzard, and which regularly reverberate to the sound of steam.

The story of the 15in gauge makes happier reading, and it is appropriate to discuss its ancestry here since its roots lie in Derbyshire, and most of these lines are in England, although its influence has extended beyond the borders. The pioneer was Sir Arthur Percival Heywood, who during the early 1870s conducted various experiments to determine the minimum gauge which could be used safely and advantageously on large country estates. In 1874, after settling for 15in, he built a proving line at his home, Duffield Bank, near Derby. Sir Arthur hoped his idea would mushroom,

but disappointingly the only other such line of any note was the Duke of Westminster's three mile line connecting Eaton Hall, near Chester, with the GWR at Balderton, which operated for 50 years from 1896. Sir Arthur constructed three engines for Duffield Bank, and a further three for Eaton Hall.

However at the beginning of this century the potentialities of the 15in for purely pleasure lines was dawning, and from 1905 Narrow Gauge Enterprises operated a number of these lines using locomotives of scale proportions to their standard gauge counterparts. Equipment was supplied mainly by the associated Northampton company, W.J. Bassett-Lowke Ltd, which specialised in the miniature railway field. With the outbreak of the first world war NGE activities were drastically curtailed, and while looking for a new site for much of its redundant equipment the proprietors discovered the then moribund Ravenglass & Eskdale Railway, leased the line, and in 1915 began conversion of the original 3ft gauge to 15in, thus heralding the start of the R&ER in its present form.

The early Bassett-Lowke locomotives, the Little Giant 4-4-2 class, were designed by Henry Greenly, a prominent journalist in the railway modelling world who exerted great influence over 15in gauge development. Greenly later met Capt J.E.P. Howey and was largely responsible for the design of the latter's Romney, Hythe & Dymchurch Railway, looked upon by many today as the ultimate in minimum gauge operating practice.

In recent times the level of narrow gauge activity in England has grown tremendously, both on the 15in and the broader gauge lines. This development, and the affection with which steam is held, can be assessed by the fact that over 160 narrow gauge locomotives can be located within the domain of St George, and that of the 23 lines and centres illustrated in the following pages 21 have been founded since 1960. Considering the sparsity of such public lines in pre-preservation days and their early demise, it is a truly remarkable achievement.

The ironstone railways of the Midlands were once the stamping ground for many narrow gauge steam locomotives, and representing this bygone era is Kettering Coal & Iron Co Ltd 3ft gauge 0-6-0ST *Kettering Furnaces No 7,* built by Manning Wardle in 1897, here labouring uphill with a heavy load of ironstone on a very wet 13 May 1960.   *(Ivo Peters)*

15in gauge survivor. On the Romney, Hythe & Dymchurch Railway, which has served Romney Marsh for over 50 years, 1926 built Davey Paxman 4-6-2 No 7 *Typhoon* leaves Dymchurch with the 16.55 Dungeness-Hythe on 17 June 1978. A touch of modernity is added by the colour light signal.

(G T Heavyside)

It is appropriate that our tour of the English narrow gauge railways should start with the 15in gauge Ravenglass & Eskdale Railway, one of England's most scenic lines and affectionately known as the Ratty, as well as being one of the oldest narrow gauge lines in Britain. Here 2-8-2 *River Mite*, built by Clarkson of York in 1966, waits to commence its journey from Ravenglass on 15 July 1978, the engine initially achieving fame when it was hauled across the Pennines from its York makers behind a traction engine. The jet of steam comes from the air brake compressor exhaust.

(G T Heavyside)

To mark 100 years of passenger carrying on the Ratty a number of 15in gauge locomotives from throughout Britain visited the railway during September 1976, although the line (originally of 3ft gauge) opened for freight in 1875. Near Beckfoot with a train from Ravenglass is Romney Hythe & Dymchurch Railway 4-6-2 No 10 *Doctor Syn* on 26 September 1976.

(D Rodgers)

On the same day another of the visitors, Bressingham Steam Museum's Krupp-built Pacific No 1662 *Rosenkavalier* heads back to Ravenglass near Fisherground loop, one of three passing points on the line, the others being at Irton Road and Miteside. *(D Rodgers)*

Left: Ready for the day's work outside Ravenglass shed on 22 July 1979 are left, Davey Paxman 2-8-2 *River Esk* of 1923, and 2-6-2 *Northern Rock* constructed at Ravenglass in 1976. The four steam engines on the R&ER burn coke and on peak days they are all pressed into service. *(G T Heavyside)*

Right: *River Esk* bridges the Whillan Beck, a tributary to the Esk, on leaving Dalegarth (since renamed Eskdale) with the 15.40 for Ravenglass on 15 July 1978.
(G T Heavyside)

Left: Nearing the Cumbrian coast towards the end of its seven-mile journey from Eskdale, *Northern Rock* passes the Ravenglass fixed distant signal on 22 July 1979. On the left is the River Mite. *(G T Heavyside)*

Right lower: On the same day, against a backcloth of a rugged Lakeland fell, 0-8-2 *River Irt* coasts towards Irton Road in charge of the 16.40 Ravenglass-Eskdale. This is the third member of the trio of engines on the Ratty named after the rivers Esk, Mite and Irt, which flow into the Irish Sea at Ravenglass through a common exit. *(G T Heavyside)*

Below: Earlier that day, with Hooker Crag rising majestically ahead, *River Irt* scrambles up the severe gradient from Muncaster Mill while hauling the 14.10 from Ravenglass. *River Irt* was built by Sir Arthur Heywood at Duffield Bank in 1894 as 0-8-0T *Muriel,* and rebuilt at Ravenglass in 1927. *(G T Heavyside)*

Above: With an exhaust that belies its size, 2-8-2 *River Esk* drags its train of open stock up the 1 in 36 Hollinghow bank leaving The Green for Eskdale on 19 July 1979. *(G T Heavyside)*

Left: The following day the same section of track is viewed from the footplate of *River Esk*, this time at the head of the 14.40 Eskdale-Ravenglass. During the journey drivers have constant contact by radio with a control room adjoining Ravenglass signalbox, from where all movements on the railway are sanctioned, a graph being maintained detailing the running movements authorised and ensuring safe operation. Approaching each passing loop drivers must report their position to control and they are then given further instructions. The system was inaugurated in May 197 and is the only British passenger-carrying line so equipped. *(G T Heavyside)*

Right: Dwarfed by its surroundings 2-8-2 *River Mit* draws its train into Eskdale (then known as Dalegarth) on 15 July 1978. The tracks leading out of the picture below are connected by a turntable, a second one being installed at Ravenglass. *(G T Heavyside)*

On 17 June 1979 Bassett-Lowke 4-4-2 No 18 of 1911 travels the 15in gauge line at Steamtown Railway Museum, Carnforth. Tracks for the numerous standard gauge exhibits maintained at this former BR motive power depot are visible behind the train, while above the driver can be seen one of the masts for the adjacent electrified West Coast main line.   (G T Heavyside)

At first glance this appears to be another of Steamtown's inhabitants — LNER A3 class Pacific No 4472 *Flying Scotsman*. It is in fact a 15in gauge scale replica of the famous East Coast main line racehorse and is seen here outside the shed at Whorlton Lido, near Barnard Castle, on 27 August 1978.   (G T Heavyside)

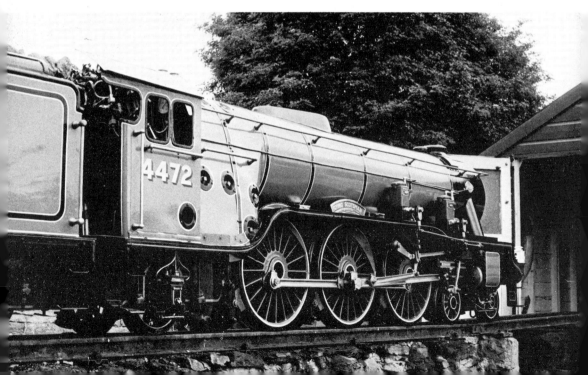

Weaving through a tree-lined section of the Whorlton
circuit with the passenger service on the same day is
1912-built Bassett-Lowke Atlantic *King George*.
(G T Heavyside)

Right: A happy crowd enjoy a trip behind ex-Penrhyn Quarries Hunslet 0-4-0ST *Alan George* (works No 606 of 1894) along the private 1ft 10¾in gauge Howden-clough Light Railway at Bruntcliffe, near Leeds, on 1 July 1979. Bringing up the rear is Hunslet diesel mechanical locomotive *Sholto.* *(G T Heavyside)*

Below: The narrow gauge is not forgotten at the National Railway Museum, York, and on 7 April 1979 the pioneer Beyer-Garratt locomotive, Beyer Peacock 0-4-0 + 0-4-0T works No 5292 built in 1909 for the 2ft gauge North East Dundas Tramway in Tasmania, stands proudly in the main exhibition hall. This historic engine is on loan from the Festiniog Railway, which acquired it from Beyer Peacock on closure of its Gorton, Manchester, factory in the mid-1960s, having been brought home in 1947. *(G T Heavyside)*

Below right: The Lincolnshire Coast Light Railway, Humberston, Cleethorpes, first ran trains in 1960 although in 1966 its 2ft wide track was completely realigned; on the new formation in 1969 Peckett 0-6-0ST *Jurassic,* of 1903 vintage, is seen on arrival at South Sea Lane terminus with an ex-Ashover Light Railway coach. *(J D Portlock)*

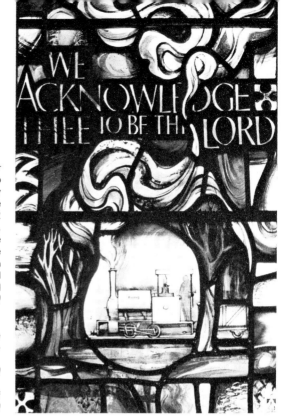

Left: The ancient parish of All Saints, Cadeby, near Market Bosworth, which can trace its history back to the thirteenth century, today boasts a 2ft gauge railway round the rectory, the line being opened in 1963 at the instigation of the rector, Rev E. R. Boston. On 12 August 1978 under the shadow of the church tower, former Northamptonshire ironstone quarry locomotive 0-4-0ST *Pixie* (Bagnall No 2090 built 1919) begins the short journey from Cadeby to Sutton Lane. Traction engines are also maintained here, while a large model railway, based on GWR practice, is housed in the shed on the left of *Pixie.*   *(G T Heavyside)*

Right: Worshippers at All Saints are reminded of the railway's close proximity by this profile of *Pixie* incorporated in the stained glass east window.
          (G T Heavyside)

Below: Rev E.R. 'Teddy' Boston on the footplate of *Pixie.*   *(G T Heavyside)*

Left: Ready for duty on the 1978 opened 1ft 10¾in gauge Thursford Steam Railway, near Fakenham, Norfolk, at an already established traction engine and organ museum, is ex-Dinorwic Slate Quarry octogenarian Hunslet 0-4-0ST *Cackler* on 16 August 1978.

(R R Darsley)

Left Centre: The unique vertical boilered engine built by Mr. D. C. Potter circa 1970, ambles along his private 2ft gauge Yaxham Park Light Railway, near East Dereham, Norfolk, on 1 July 1978.　　(R R Darsley)

Right: Famed for its fine collection of standard gauge engines, Bressingham Steam Museum in the grounds of horticulturist Alan Bloom at Diss, Norfolk, also hosts a fleet of narrow gauge locomotives. On 24 June 1973 on 60cm gauge track Alan Bloom is seen at the controls of Hudswell Clarke 0-6-0WT *Bronllwyd*.　　(G T Monks)

Right lower: On the same day on similar gauge track Hunslet 0-4-0ST with tender *Gwynedd* works No 316 of 1883 (but shorn of nameplates) prepares to traverse a different circuit through the Bressingham nurseries.

(G T Monks)

Below: Motive power on Bressingham's 2¼ mile 15in gauge Waveney Valley Railway circuit is provided by two Krupp-built Pacifics imported from West Germany in 1972. Here No 1662 *Rosenkavalier* gets a train under way in August 1974.　　(J R Smith)

Above: On the 2ft gauge Leighton Buzzard Narrow Gauge Railway Kerr Stuart Wren class 0-4-0ST No 2 *Pixie* crosses another train at Leedon Loop while heading for Page's Park on 3 September 1978.

(*G T Heavyside*)

Below: Traffic is halted while vertical boilered De Winton 0-4-0T No 1 *Chaloner* is flagged safely across Stanbridge Road with a well filled train on the LBNGR in May 1972. This former North Wales quarry locomotive celebrated its centenary during 1977. (*R L Patrick*)

Right upper: Rescued from India in 1971 Baguley 0-4-0T No 3 *Rishra* now graces the one-time sand carrying LBNGR and is pictured here shortly after leaving Stonehenge on 28 April 1973. (*G T Monks*)

Right lower: Lure of steam! Two youngsters gaze intently at 0-4-0WT No 11 *P C Allen* at Page's Park during August 1971. The engine was built by the German company Orenstein & Koppel in 1912 and arrived in England in 1963 after spending its commercial life at a Spanish chemical works. (*G D King*)

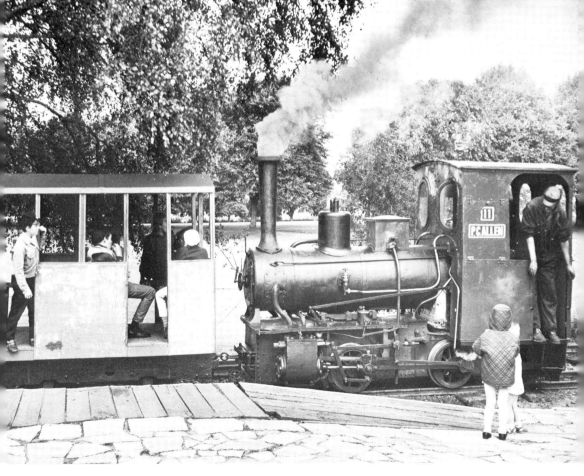

Above: Four 2ft 6in gauge steam locomotives formerly used by Bowaters at Sittingbourne have in recent years found employment at Whipsnade Zoo, Dunstable, on the Whipsnade & Umfolozi Railway which offers passengers close views of white rhinos, bison, camels, and other mammals in open surroundings. Here No 3 Bagnall 0-6-2T *Conqueror* rouses the echoes as it leaves the station on 3 September 1978.

(G T Heavyside)

Right upper: On 28 May 1973 No 1 Manning Wardle 0-6-2T *Chevallier* storms away at the start of another tour of the Whipsnade animal paddocks while on the right *Conqueror* waits to leave with the next train which will complete the circuit in the opposite direction. Although a short section was in use from August 1970 the line had an official royal opening by HRH Princess Margaret on 2 August 1973.

(G T Monks

Right lower: Contrasting sharply with the operational railway at Whipsnade on 3 September 1978 is 3ft 6in gauge Sharp Stewart 4-8-0 No 390 (works No 4150 of 1896) and a former Rhodesian Railways coach which were imported from the Zambesi Sawmills Railway, Zambia, in 1975 by renowned wildlife artist and conservationist David Shepherd.

(G T Heavyside

On special occasions the 1ft 11½in gauge Knebworth West Park & Wintergreen Railway, in the grounds of Knebworth House, near Stevenage, Hertfordshire, has played host to visiting locomotives, while at the same time steaming the resident engines. One such event was held in conjunction with a Wonderful World of Wheels exhibition staged by the Transport Trust on 2 September 1978, when the photographs on these two pages were taken.

Above: Hunslet 0-4-0ST *Lilla* of 1891 vintage bides time during a journey along the Knebworth track.
(G T Heavyside)

Below: Avonside 0-4-0T *Sezela No 4,* imported from Natal, South Africa, in 1976, takes its turn on the passenger service. *(G T Heavyside)*

Lilla blasts away from the main station and passes one of the visitors, Kerr Stuart Wren class 0-4-0ST *Peter Pan* resting between duties. *(G T Heavyside)*

Regular inhabitant Hunslet 0-4-0ST No 1 (works No 1429 of 1922) trundles back towards Knebworth House. *(G T Heavyside)*

Kerr Stuart 0-4-2ST *Premier* draws away from Kemsley Down on the 2ft 6in gauge Sittingbourne & Kemsley Railway on 18 June 1978. The large pipes framing *Premier* and which accompany the railway belong to the line's previous operator, Bowater's United Kingdom Pulp & Paper Mills Ltd, and convey steam from its Kemsley mill to Sittingbourne mill.   *(G T Heavyside*

Premier cautiously crosses the reinforced concrete viaduct at the approach to Sittingbourne with the stock which will form the first public train of the day on 18 June 1978.   *(G T Heavyside)*

Bagnall 0-6-2T *Triumph* en route for Sittingbourne with the 13.20 from Kemsley Down on 13 August 1970. The balloon stack chimneys, which give the engines an overseas appearance, originally carried spark arresting apparatus, an essential requirement during the years the railway served the paper industry.   *(D A Idle)*

Romneyrail - Main Line Practice

The Romney, Hythe & Dymchurch Railway, often referred to as the world's smallest public railway, was the brainchild of Capt J.E.P. Howey, whose aspirations to operate a scaled down version of a main line railway materialised with the opening of the initial section of this 15in gauge line along the Kent coast between Hythe and New Romney in July 1927. A year later the 13.8 mile route was complete when the Dungeness extension opened. Howey remained principal shareholder until his death in 1963, whereupon followed some difficult years before the present management took control in 1972, but while many changes have occurred Howey's basic philosophies still hold sway.

Unusually for the narrow gauge a double track route was laid, although after derequisitioning by the Army following the second world war, the New Romney to Dungeness section was singled. Turntables were installed at New Romney, Hythe, and Dymchurch, the first two still being used, and with a balloon loop at Dungeness engines are thus always able to haul trains running in a forward direction, which is a pleasant change from the tender/bunker first running seen on most lines.

For motive power the Romney relies mainly on nine steam locomotives built for the line between 1925 and 1931. The first seven were constructed by Davey Paxman of Colchester, comprising five Pacifics based on Gresley's original A1 design for the Great Northern Railway (later LNER A3 class) and two 4-8-2s, all built to one third scale rather than the more accurate quarter scale for the gauge. The other two engines, both Pacifics, have a typical North American outline, complete with cow-catchers, and were built by the Yorkshire Engine Co. In 1976 the stock was augmented by a Krupp built Pacific of the 1930s imported from Germany, and since named *Black Prince*.

Operation is centred on New Romney and during the high season the station despatches 24 trains daily, 17 to Hythe and seven for Dungeness, and sees a similar number of arrivals. With shunting movements, and engines going on and off shed, the scene here often resembles such places as Bournemouth Central and Newton Abbot in the heyday of steam!

In 1979 during late July and August the timetable provided for trains at half hourly intervals (except Saturdays) from late morning until early evening between New Romney and Hythe, with seven forming through workings to and from Dungeness, while on Fridays there was an extra early morning train from New Romney on the Dungeness line. Saturdays saw 12 return workings to Hythe and seven to Dungeness but additionally there was a non-stop train, The Golden Jubilee, from Hythe to Dungeness and back with a 42min schedule each way, compared with 80min for all other

Left: One of the Canadian outline engines, No 10 *Doctor Syn* leaves New Romney shed, while on the right fellow Pacific No 8 *Hurricane* awaits its next turn of duty on 14 June 1978. *(G T Heavyside)*

Above right: Diagram (not to scale) of main station areas on Romney, Hythe & Dymchurch Railway.

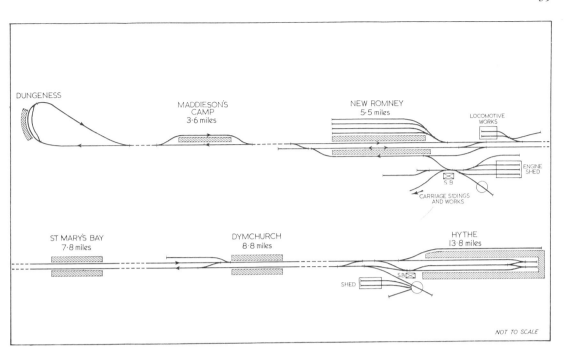

trains which stopped at the principal stations, and by request at three halts on the Dungeness extension.

The peak service required six locomotives in traffic daily, the most arduous duty covering three return trips to Hythe and two to Dungeness, journeys totalling 72 miles. Cumulatively the engines registered 360 miles per day (over 370 on Fridays), a notable feat for a 15in gauge line. During this period at least eight engines were needed in working order, for at the end of a six-day cycle another two were required for boiler washouts and essential maintenance. That this intensive service was operated with only 10 suitable passenger engines speaks volumes for the high standard of workmanship.

Train frequency is normally increased from March in line with demand, and eased off after August (being week-ends only at the extremities of the operating season) although throughout the year during term-time, a schools service is run from Burmarsh Road, one mile north-east of Dymchurch, to New Romney. In addition specials are organised for various parties, while in recent years a few express Hythe to Hythe via Dungeness journeys have been enjoyed by visiting railway enthusiasts.

Signalling is also to main line standards, with movements at New Romney authorised from a 24 lever fully interlocked signalbox, while a similar 16 lever box controls the station precincts at Hythe. Between these points trains run under absolute block, with block posts at St Mary's Bay and Dymchurch. Safe operation of the single line Dungeness extension is ensured by the staff and ticket method, the only crossing loop being at Maddieson's Camp, which was installed during the winter of 1973-4 to facilitate an hourly frequency on this section.

Over the years the Romney has kept pace with modern technology, colour-light signals, some with route indicators, now controlling the line, although a link with the past is maintained at Hythe where a semaphore gantry governs the exit from the platforms. Recently all the level crossings on the Hythe route have been protected by flashing light traffic signals for road users, which are activated automatically by approaching trains through track circuits.

Today the RH&DR carries more than 350,000 passengers a year, the majority holiday-makers and day-trippers, but others, like the schoolchildren, use the railway for convenience. A visit to the line is a joy, with the spotless engines, meticulously cared for by their regular drivers, hauling rakes of coaches at scale speeds of over 70mph. Here one can relish again the great traditions of the old main line companies which are still perpetuated across the flats of Romney Marsh.

Right: Painted in LNER green, Pacific No 3 *Southern Maid* reposes within the cavernous Hythe station after arrival from New Romney on 15 June 1978.
(G T Heavyside)

Below: Nocturnal view of Krauss 0-4-0 No 4 *The Bug* at Hythe in September 1976. The engine was used during construction of the line but not being powerful enough for ordinary services was sold to a Blackpool pleasure line in 1933. It subsequently found its way to Belfast from where, after spending over 20 years in a scrapyard, it was fortuitously rescued in 1972. On returning home it was restored to working order and now sees occasional use on special trains.
(A R W Crowhurst)

Below right: The Hythe turntable is locked into position while the driver oils the motion of 4-8-2 No 5 *Hercules* during the summer of 1973. (A R W Crowhurst)

The fictional character Doctor Syn, the vicar of Dymchurch cum smuggler portrayed in Russell Thorndike's novels, will never die while Pacific No 10 continues to roam across Romney Marsh! *Doctor Syn* is seen here steaming past the colour-light signal protecting the approach to New Romney station with the 12.50 Dungeness-Hythe on 14 June 1978.   *(G T Heavyside)*

On the same day the other Canadian outline locomotive 4-6-2 No 9 *Winston Churchill* is reflected in the waters beneath Botolph's Bridge while hauling the 15.20 Hythe-Dungeness.   *(G T Heavyside)*

The prototype RH&DR Pacific No 1 *Green Goddess* approaches Dymchurch with a train for Hythe in August 1976.   *(A R W Crowhurst)*

The old lighthouse stands guard as Pacific No 7 *Typhoon* leaves Dungeness on a sultry afternoon in June 1978. Like their GNR counterparts *Typhoon* and sister locomotive *Hurricane* were built with three cylinders, but were not entirely satisfactory in this form and by 1937 both had had the inside cylinder removed. A new lighthouse (hidden by the train) was built when the one depicted was partly obscured from the sea by the adjoining nuclear power station.   *(G T Heavyside)*

Above: Brockham Museum, Betchworth, near Dorking, Surrey, was founded during the 1960s to display various facets of the narrow gauge, and nearing completion of a major overhaul on 6 May 1979 is 2ft gauge 2-4-0T *Polar Bear,* built by Bagnall in 1905. Before arrival here in 1967 the engine had spent its entire working life on the Groudle Glen Railway, Isle of Man.
(D H Smith)

Right: In pristine condition Andrew Barclay 0-4-0WT No 1 *Caledonia* jogs along the 2ft gauge Hollycombe Woodland Railway, Liphook, Hants, on 11 June 1978. Note the bullhead keyed track. Other Hollycombe attractions include standard gauge locomotives, traction engines, a steam powered fairground, and demonstrations of ways in which steam was at one time used in agriculture.
(G T Heavyside)

Left: Cabless Hunslet Alice class 0-4-0ST *Cloister* (works No 542 of 1891) basks in the afternoon sunshine on the Hampshire Narrow Gauge Railway Society's 2ft gauge line at Durley, near Southampton, on 10 April 1976, a far cry from hauling slate trucks at Dinorwic Quarries in North Wales! *(Ivo Peters)*

Below left: Another view of *Cloister* at Durley, this time at work on 11 September 1976. *(M Wood)*

Below: On the 15in gauge Longleat Light Railway, at Longleat Park, near Warminster, opened in 1965, a location perhaps more noted for its safari park, 0-6-2T *Dougal* and 0-6-0 *Muffin* pose for the camera on 4 July 1970. Neither engine has yet reached the age of maturity, *Dougal* being built by Severn-Lamb in 1970 and *Muffin* by Berwyn in 1967. *Muffin* has since transferred its affections to the Lappa Valley Railway in Cornwall. *(Ivo Peters)*

Above: Bicton Gardens, near Budleigh Salterton, Devon, were designed by the French landscape artist Andre le Notre and laid out in 1735, but it wasn't until the early 1960s that the public gained admittance. Since 1963 visitors have also been able to enjoy the delights of the 1ft 6in gauge Bicton Woodland Railway and on 26 July 1966 0-4-0T *Woolwich,* built in 1916 by Avonside for the Royal Arsenal at Woolwich, threads the gardens with a well filled train.　　*(Ivo Peters)*

Top right: Amputated from the British Rail netwo under Dr Beeching, the Chacewater to Newquay line Cornwall has been partly restored to health by the ope ing in 1974 of the 15in gauge Lappa Valley Railwa which utilises a section of this former Great Weste highway at Newlyn East. Sitting where Churchward ar Collett locomotives used to roam is Severn-Lar 1974-built 0-6-2T *Zebedee* at East Wheal Rose Mi with a train for Benny Halt on 23 September 1977.
(M Woo

Right: On the same day *Zebedee* lingers awhile on t turntable at Benny Halt.　　*(M Woo*

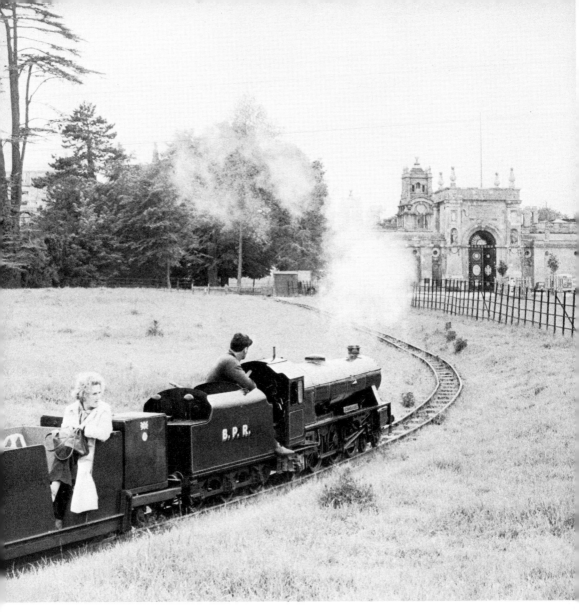

Situated in the grounds of Blenheim Palace, Woodstock near Oxford, home of the Duke of Marlborough and birthplace of Sir Winston Churchill, is a 15in gauge railway, and running towards the palace on 8 June 1978 is 4-6-2 *Sir Winston Churchill*, originally built as 4-6-0 by G & S Light Engineering of Stourbridge for Dudley Zoo in 1946. The engine was previously known as *Prince Charles*, being re-named after Blenheim's famous statesman on coming here for the opening of the line in 1975. *(G T Heavyside)*

Looking forward to active days again at the Northamptonshire Ironstone Railway Trust, Hunsbury Hill, near Northampton, during 1978, is metre gauge Peckett 0-6-0ST No 87 works No 2029 of 1942. The engine previously worked at Finedon ironstone quarries, near Wellingborough. Notice the metre gauge track interlaced with that of standard gauge. *(R L Patrick)*

Scotland

Bonnie Scotland with its vast areas of mountains, moors, and lochs, coupled with a population which outside the Forth-Clyde industrial belt, and a few other centres, is decidedly thin on the ground, would appear to have been an ideal place for the development of narrow gauge rails. Perhaps surprisingly the land of the clans has fared worse in this respect than any other country in the British Isles.

North of Hadrian's Wall the only public railway built with track less than standard width was the 2ft 3in gauge Campbeltown & Machrihanish Light Railway, near the foot of the lonely Kintyre peninsula. This line started life in 1906, being partly laid on the course of an earlier colliery line, but within 26 years its services had been expunged and the stock placed at the mercy of a scrap-merchant.

Scottish industrialists have made some use of the narrow gauge, but the majority of steam engines which worked these tracks long ago followed the path of their Kintyre brethren, and in consequence only a handful can currently be found in the country, and none of these, at the time of writing, are publicly steamed.

However one bright spot is in the Grampian region, where work progresses on building the 2ft gauge Alford Valley Railway from Bridge of Alford to the former Great North of Scotland Railway Alford station, and steam traction is envisaged in the near future. May its life be long and as successful as some of its contemporaries in other parts of the British Isles.

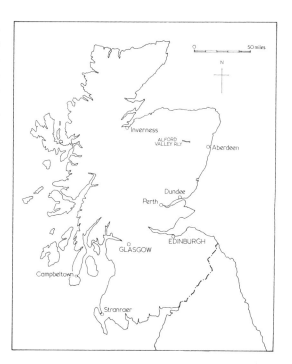

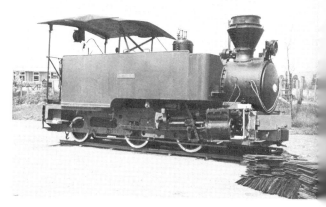

Far from its previous home on the South African Cane Growers Association Mount Edgecombe Plantation, Natal, 1934-built Fowler 0-4-2T *Saccearine* stands on an isolated piece of track in its new surroundings on the Alford Valley Railway, following its arrival in Scotland during April 1979. *(F S Munro)*

Wales

The people of Wales are famed for their musical talents and love of rugby, while in many areas the native language is still widely used despite the country having been politically and administratively linked with England for centuries. The land west of Offa's Dyke is noted too for its coastal beauty and mountainous terrain, and in recent years the narrow gauge railways which abound in North and Mid Wales have also come to be regarded with affection by many visitors.

The Principality is indeed the cradle of narrow gauge steam for, as outlined in the introduction, it was the Festiniog Railway which in 1863 introduced the iron horse to so narrow a gauge as 1ft 11½in, and two years later it became the first authorised to carry fare paying passengers. However the travelling public was not the Festiniog's life-blood, the line originally being opened in 1836 to transport slate mined from the rich deposits around Blaenau Ffestiniog over the 13 difficult miles to Porthmadog, from where it was widely distributed via the harbour. The wagons in pre-steam days descended to the coast by gravity, while horses hauled them back.

The seemingly insatiable demand for slate during the nineteenth century led to the construction of other lines in the northern half of Wales, including some very extensive systems, among them the network which served the vast Dinorwic Quarries at Llanberis, once one of the largest in the world. Here at its peak, on galleries stepped in the mountainside, were some 50 miles of 1ft 10¾in gauge track, the slate trucks being lowered by a system of rope-worked inclines to Llanberis, where they were placed aboard transporter wagons to reach the coast at Port Dinorwic by the 4ft gauge Padarn Railway.

Dinorwic Quarry closed in 1969 but its memory will not easily be obliterated, for in addition to the gigantic scars left ingrained on the mountainside, much of the original atmosphere of this once thriving place has been retained in the quarry workshops which now host the North Wales Quarrying Museum. Railways have not been forgotten and among the exhibits is Hunslet 0-4-0ST *Una,* although this engine formerly worked at Pen-Yr-Orsedd Quarry, Nantlle. Steam has also reappeared along a section of Padarn Railway trackbed on the 197? opened 1ft 11½in gauge Llanberis Lake Railway, and which numbers some ex-Dinorwic engines among its stock.

Returning to the last century, the advent of steam on the slate lines unfortunately came a little late for the quarry and mine owners to obtain maximum benefit from this source of power, for from the 1880s demand for their product began to decline, until today the industry is but a shadow of its former self. However the same mountains which served the local population by yielding their contents were then beginning to attract, through their inherent beauty, an increasing number of visitors to the area, and making no small contribution to the growth of what is now one of the country's main industries — tourism. Many lines, not all of which owed their birth to slate, were soon looking to these visitors as an opportunity of earning some much needed extra revenue, even so the first half of the twentieth century was a difficult time for the narrow gauge, some lines eventually succumbing to the inevitable while others eked out a bare existence.

The introduction to this book refers to the historic events of October 1950 which led to the continuance of the otherwise defunct Talyllyn Railway, and how within a few years the Festiniog had likewise been resuscitated by preservationists, while the Welshpool & Llanfair was similarly revived in 1963. During this period the Snowdon Mountain, Fairbourne and the British Rail owned Vale of Rheidol lines continued to operate on a commercial basis and since then these six lines have gone from strength to strength.

Although a friendly spirit of rivalry exists between partisans of some concerns they have in recent years worked very closely together their mutual benefit, while at the same time

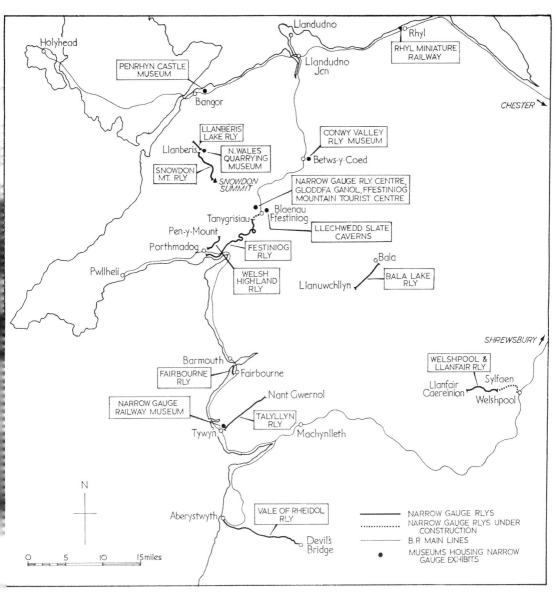

carefully retaining their individuality. In 1970 these six lines formed a Joint Marketing Panel, later being joined by the Llanberis Lake and Bala Lake railways, and have since become universally known under the corporate title The Great Little Trains of Wales. Posters and timetables are published giving details of the lines and a publicity film *Land of the Little Trains* has been produced, while a weekly season ticket is available allowing unlimited travel on all lines except the Snowdon Mountain. From 1979 literature has also advertised some non-steam lines.

Recent years have seen a further growth of the narrow gauge, for following the 1976 Talyllyn extension from Abergynolwyn to Nant Gwernol, 1977 saw Festiniog trains proceeding beyond Dduallt for the first time for over 30 years, while 1978 saw the return of 15in gauge steam to Rhyl — one of its early haunts. By now a rejuvenated Welsh Highland, after almost 20 years' work, had hoped to have joined the ranks of the operating lines, with a section from Porthmadog again carrying trains, but the manifestation of the aims of its supporters should not now be long delayed.

Under a mountain of slate at Llanberis, Dinorwic Quarries cabless Hunslet 0-4-0ST *George B* greets fellow Hunslet 0-4-0ST *Cackler* on 26 June 1956. Both engines have been preserved, *George B* at the Dowty Railway Preservation Society depot, Ashchurch, Gloucestershire, while *Cackler* operates services on the Thursford Steam Railway in Norfolk. *(Ivo Peters)*

At present this expansion shows no sign of abating, for during the early 1980s the Festiniog hopes to extend still further to its final destination in the heart of Blaenau Ffestiniog to a new Central station to be shared with BR and which, as can be seen from the map, will re-establish a second rail route to the West Coast of Wales, albeit necessitating a change of gauge twice if travelling beyond Porthmadog! An equally ambitious project is the Welshpool & Llanfair's bid to reinstate trains to the one mile 1 in 30 Golfa incline and to terminate services at a new station on the outskirts of Welshpool, as it is no longer possible to re-lay the remainder of the original route through the town to the BR station. There is talk in the air of extending the Bala Lake Railway nearer Bala itself, while narrow gauge steam locomotives have begun infiltrating South Wales, at Pontsticill, near Merthyr Tydfil.

As well as offering their customers an opportunity of enjoying steam travel the lines provide a convenient way (in some cases the only one) of savouring some of the exquisite beauty of Wales, the combined attractions bringing such a deluge of humanity that at peak periods it has sometimes been difficult for them to keep pace with their growth in popularity. In recognition of their efforts in promoting tourism the railways have received various awards from the Wales Tourist Board, both collectively and individually. They also serve the community by providing full time employment for many people.

The importance of the narrow gauge in the history of Wales cannot be over-estimated, and, rightfully, various museums display facets of the subject. It is pleasing to report that, in all, over 80 narrow gauge steam engines can be located within the Principality, including many ex-quarry locomotives, these forming a worthy tribute to the past while simultaneously continuing to serve their country in their modern environment. *Bydded i chwi lwyddo a thyfu chwi drenau bychain Cymru* (May ye prosper and grow, ye Great Little Trains of Wales).

56

Throughout the commercial life of the Welshpool & Llanfair Railway, which lasted 53 years from 1903, first as an independent concern operated by the Cambrian Railway, and later under Great Western and British Railways ownership, only two steam engines ever plied its 2ft 6in wide tracks. 1963 witnessed the line's revival using the same two engines, *The Earl* and *The Countess,* but in recent times they have been joined by locomotives and coaches imported from various corners of the world, giving the railway a very cosmopolitan flavour.

Right: On 27 May 1973 0-6-0T *The Earl* strolls by the River Banwy, just west of Heniarth, with a train for Llanfair Caereinion.   *(G T Heavyside)*

Below: Near the same spot on 2 June 1979, during an afternoon of driving rain, Hunslet 1954-built 2-6-2T No 85 makes for Llanfair. The engine and rear coach came from Sierra Leone, while the coach sandwiched between formerly worked on the Zillertalbahn Railway in Austria.   *(G T Heavyside)*

Below right: Sauntering along on a bright afternoon in 1969 is *The Earl's* twin sister 0-6-0T *The Countess.* Both engines were constructed by Beyer Peacock in 1902.   *(L A Nixon)*

The old order remaineth — or so it would appear! From 1931 until its demise in 1956 the W&LR was purely a freight carrying line, and at an Enthusiasts' Day on 14 May 1978 the atmosphere of those halcyon days is recreated by *The Earl,* here about to leave Cyfronydd with a demonstration goods train. *The Earl* is presently on loan to the National Railway Museum, York.

(R E B Siviter)

W&LR 0-6-2T *Joan* leads the 17.05 Sylfaen-Llanfair Caereinion along a section of track near Cyfronydd that looks rather akin to her previous tropical home in Antigua, in the West Indies, on 19 August 1978. *Joan* was built in 1927 by Kerr Stuart for the Antigua Sugar Co, and repatriated in 1971.

(G T Heavyside)

Another foreign looking locomotive, although coming from no further away than Bowaters at Sittingbourne, Bagnall 0-4-4-0T *Monarch,* works No 3024 of 1953, forges away from Sylfaen on 6 October 1973. Some of the cattle look more bemused by the photographer!

(R E B Siviter)

Built as an 0-8-0 tender locomotive by Société Franco-Belge in 1944 for the German Military Railways, No 699.01 was converted to an 0-8-0T during its subsequent days with the Styrian Government Railway, Austria. Following its arrival on the Welshpool in 1969 it was named *Sir Drefaldwyn* (Welsh for Montgomery-shire) and is seen here arriving at Llanfair Caereinion during August 1972. A breath of the GWR is provided by the lower quadrant signals. *(G D King)*

Left: Once it was the engines of the mighty Great Western that stalked the eastern shore of Bala Lake on their journeys between Ruabon and Barmouth Junction (later renamed Morfa Mawddach); today it is engines of the Hunslet Alice class that with no less dignity tread the same footsteps along the 4½ mile section between the former Bala Junction and Llanuwchllyn. BR last used the route in January 1965 whereupon the latter section was taken over by the Bala Lake Railway which laid rails to a width of 1ft 11½in, and under the new regime ex-Dinorwic Quarries Hunslet 0-4-0ST *Maid Marion* darkens the sky at Llangower while departing for Llanuwchllyn on 16 September 1978. Great Western purists will look askance at the many Lancashire & Yorkshire Railway signal fittings in use on the line, such as these L&YR siding signal arms mounted on a GWR post at Llangower. *(G T Heavyside)*

Below: Former Dinorwic stablemate Hunslet 0-4-0ST *Holy War* scurries by Bala Lake, the largest natural expanse of water in Wales, with the 16.35 Bala-Llanuwchllyn on 29 May 1979. Like those of its illustrious predecessor the leading coaches are finished in chocolate and cream. *(G T Heavyside)*

The trackbed by Llanberis Lake used to be the preserve of slate being hauled from Dinorwic Quarries to Port Dinorwic along the 4ft gauge Padarn Railway, but since 1971 it is tourists who have warmed to the splendour of the Snowdon massif while travelling the first two miles of the route from Llanberis on 1ft 11½in wide track put down by the Llanberis Lake Railway.

Left: Built for Dinorwic Quarries in 1889, Hunslet 0-4-0ST *Elidir* skirts Llanberis Lake shortly after leaving Llanberis Padarn Park (Gilfach Ddu) on 30 May 1979.
(G T Heavyside)

Right: On the same day another locomotive from the adjacent quarries, Hunslet 0-4-0ST *Dolbadarn* sojourns at Cei Llydan during a torrential downpour, before continuing to Llanberis. *(G T Heavyside)*

Right lower: *Elidir* chugs along the water's edge with a Llanberis to Penllyn train on 10 September 1978.
(G T Heavyside)

Below: From much further afield, German import Jung 0-4-0WT, works No 7509 of 1937, and since named *Ginette Marie,* rounds a curve near Penllyn heading for Llanberis on 31 May 1975. *(L A Nixon)*

Sic itur ad astra — such is the way to the stars — is the motto of the 2ft 7½in (800mm) gauge Snowdon Mountain Railway, which clambers from Llanberis almost to the 3560ft summit of Snowdon (the highest mountain in Wales) by means of the solitary Swiss Abt rack-rail system laid in Britain. Eight 0-4-2Ts, which take their drive through the rack pinions, were built for the line between 1895 and 1923 by Schweizerische Lokomotiv & Maschinenfabrik, Winterthur, Switzerland, although No 1 was tragically lost in an 1896 opening day accident, which delayed further services for another year while additional safety measures were taken.

Above: On 12 September 1978 No 8 *Eryri* slowly descends the lower reaches of Snowdon returning to Llanberis; maximum permitted speed in either direction is 5mph. *(G T Heavyside)*

Left: No 2 *Enid* comes off the 14 arch Lower viaduct shortly after leaving Llanberis on 30 May 1979. Coaches remain uncoupled throughout the journey. *(G T Heavyside)*

Right: After taking sustenance at Halfway, No 4 *Snowdon* prepares to resume battle with the ferocious mountain gradients, as steep as 1 in 5½ in places, on 12 September 1978. *(G T Heavyside)*

Above: Against a rocky Snowdonia background No 7 *Aylwin* (since renamed *Ralph Sadler*), with seemingly steam to spare, pushes its one coach towards the summit on 12 September 1978. Notice the barricade in the cab doorway protecting the crew from the elements, the winds sometimes becoming so strong as to prevent running on the upper section. *(G T Heavyside)*

Top left: Earlier the same day *Aylwin* waits in the loop at Halfway as No 4 *Snowdon* grinds slowly up grade. *(G T Heavyside)*

Left: A scene not witnessed by many visitors to Snowdon — the hazards of winter maintenance. With the engineers train near the summit is No 5 *Moel Siabod* on 8 November 1967. *(P J Fowler)*

Right: After a day's toil on the mountain No 8 *Eryri* has its smokebox and tubes cleaned outside Llanberis shed on 12 September 1978. Seen clearly is the slope on the boiler which assumes a more horizontal position when on the mountain, enabling the water level to be kept above the firebox crown. *(G T Heavyside)*

Left: The doyen of narrow gauge steam railways — the 1ft 11½ in gauge Festiniog Railway. Here the second engine built for the line in 1863, George England 0-4-0ST plus tender *Prince* approaches Tan-y-Bwlch with a train from Porthmadog in July 1968. During the journey all carriage doors are locked due to very limited clearances. *(L A Nixon)*

Below left: The Festiniog is famed for its use of double-ended locomotives built to Robert Fairlie's patent, having two boilers and engine units, with a central firebox, highly suited to the line in its heavy slate-carrying days. Constructed in the FR Boston Lodge Works in 1879, Fairlie 0-4-4-0T *Merddin Emrys* sets out from Porthmadog across the Traeth Mawr embankment (known as the Cob) with the 15.00 to Tanygrisiau on 17 September 1979. *(G T Heavyside)*

Above: Hunslet 2-4-0ST plus tender *Blanche* gets into her stride on leaving Boston Lodge with the 12.30 Porthmadog-Tanygrisiau on 11 September 1978. *Blanche* and her identical twin *Linda* were built by Hunslet in 1893, works Nos 589 and 590, as 0-4-0STs for the Penrhyn Quarry Railway, being rebuilt as 2-4-0STs by the Festiniog, who also added the tenders to provide extra fuel and watering capacity. The fourth coach is also a link with the past for it is a former Lynton & Barnstaple Railway vehicle rescued by the FR and restored as a buffet car. The other coaches have been built new in the last two decades. *(G T Heavyside)*

Below: The mountains beckon as *Linda* leaves Penrhyn for Tanygrisiau on 18 September 1979. In order to combat the problem of lineside fires in forestry areas *Linda* was converted to oil-burning in 1970, and all the FR engines now run on this fuel. *(G T Heavyside)*

Top left: Nameplates of Festiniog newcomer Fairlie 0-4-4-0T *Iarll Meirionnydd/Earl of Merioneth* built at Boston Lodge in 1979, the Welsh and English versions being carried on opposite sides.

Centre left: Porthmadog recedes into the distance as *Iarll Meirionnydd/Earl of Merioneth* nears Boston Lodge along the Cob on 18 September 1979.

Above: Another view of *Iarll Meirionnydd/Earl of Merioneth* on the same day, leaving Minffordd with the 2.43 Tanygrisiau-Porthmadog.

Left: As *Linda* rolls into Dduallt from Tanygrisiau on 29 May 1979, her fireman and the signalman demonstrate the art of exchanging single line tokens, while American Locomotive Co 2-6-2T *Mountaineer* waits for the road.

Right: Not far from the Festiniog at Blaenau Ffestiniog is the 1978 established Narrow Gauge Railway Centre at Gloddfa Ganol, the Ffestiniog Mountain Tourist Centre, located at a former slate mine which once provided business for the FR. One of a galaxy of engines on display is 60cm gauge Kerr Stuart 0-6-0T works No 4451 of 1951, photographed on a wet 28 May 1979.
(All G T Heavyside)

Right: Between 1955 and 1968 the Festiniog was reopened in stages from Porthmadog to Dduallt, but, beyond, part of the original route was submerged by a reservoir serving the hydro-electric Ffestiniog Power Station — effectively blocking further progress towards Blaenau Ffestiniog, and the cause of a long legal battle with the CEGB regarding compensation. Undeterred, an entirely new 2¾ mile line was constructed at a higher level, commencing with a spiral at Dduallt, and on to Tanygrisiau, the present terminus, a stretch opened throughout in 1978. In this view on 29 May 1979 the grandeur of the FR is apparent as *Merddin Emrys* overlooks the reservoir, returning to Porthmadog from Tanygrisiau. The original route can be seen in the water just above the engine. *(G T Heavyside)*

Below: Earlier the same day *Mountaineer* hurries away from Minffordd making for Tanygrisiau. Notice the three-aspect colour-light signal, contrasting somewhat with the somersault signal on page 68! *(G T Heavyside)*

Below right: Again on 29 May 1979 *Mountaineer* circles the Dduallt spiral — the only one in Britain — with the 12.30 Porthmadog-Tanygrisiau, having just crossed the path by which it arrived at Dduallt from Tan-y-Bwlch, the smoke obliterating the bridge.
(G T Heavyside)

Now over 60 years old the 15in gauge Fairbourne Railway operates trains from Fairbourne across the sand dunes to the southern bank of the Mawddach estuary, where passengers may take the ferry to Barmouth. Under the driver's watchful eye, Pacific *Ernest W Twining,* named after the designer and built by G & S Light Engineering of Stourbridge in 1949, leaves Fairbourne on 2 June 1979. *(G T Heavyside)*

Picking its way through the sand dunes, teenager 2-4-2 *Sian,* a Twining design constructed by Guest's of Stourbridge in 1963, chatters away from Barmouth Ferry tender first on 14 September 1978. *(G T Heavyside)*

Standing at Fairbourne station cum shed on 16 September 1978 are, left, Bassett-Lowke 4-4-2 *Count Louis,* overshadowed by big sister *Katie,* another Guest-built 2-4-2 in 1954. *(G T Heavyside)*

Sian takes the curve onto the Barmouth Bay coast with a train from Fairbourne on 14 September 1978. In addition to tourists many local residents use the railway and ferry as a useful alternative to BR's Cambrian Coast line across Barmouth Bridge, a long detour being necessary by road. *(G T Heavyside)*

Footplate to Nant Gwernol

Thursday 14 September 1978 was for me no ordinary day, for by kind permission of the Talyllyn Railway management I was to travel on the footplate of the 10.00 from Tywyn Wharf to Nant Gwernol. The morning dawned warm and bright and expectantly I made my way to Tywyn Pendre, the railway's operating headquarters, there to be warmly greeted by driver Phil Care, a regular Talyllyn employee, and volunteer fireman John Burton of Bristol, who had virtually completed preparation of the engine *Sir Haydn*.

It was fitting that my journey was to be by this Hughes of Loughborough built ex-Corris Railway 0-4-2ST, celebrating its centenary year, and named after the line's previous owner, the former Merioneth MP Sir Henry Haydn Jones. Sir Haydn owned the TR, which he pledged to operate during his lifetime, and Bryn Eglwys slate quarry, the *raison d'être* for the line's existence, from 1911 to his death in 1950.

With everything in order and five coaches behind we rumbled along the single line to Wharf where, after running round our train, we patiently awaited departure time, while intending passengers admired our charge. With a good fire and 130 lb/sq in pressure in the boiler we received the green flag at ten o'clock precisely; with a short hoot on the whistle, driver Care eased open the regulator and we retraced our steps through the cutting to Pendre, *Sir Haydn* working hard on the initial stiff climb.

Once clear of the numerous railway buildings at Pendre we left urbanisation behind, and traversed a section of open countryside to the pine shrouded station at Rhydyronen (2¼ miles), before continuing the climb for another mile to Brynglas, where we stopped in the loop just short of the platform. Here fireman Burton reported our position to Tywyn from a small ground frame box, deposited the electric key token for the single line section from Pendre, and removed one that gave us authority to proceed through the next to Quarry Sidings.

Now firmly entrenched in the Afon Fathew valley and hugging its southern slopes we resumed the climb, *Sir Haydn* under driver Care's deft handling confidently hauling his train at a steady 15mph, while fireman Burton's maxim of 'little and often' maintained boiler pressure at 120 lb/sq in. On this section I was enthralled by the magnificent surroundings, dominated to the north east by the solid mass of Cader Idris (2927ft and the highest peak in the area), a view suddenly lost as we entered a wooded stretch and slowed for the three arch Dolgoch viaduct, at the approach to Dolgoch Falls station (5 miles). Here *Sir Haydn* took welcome refreshment while the guard attended to station duties.

Soon we were moving again, and after a brief halt in the 1969 installed loop at Quarry Sidings arrived at Abergynolwyn (6½ miles), for 110 years the limit of passenger operation. In recent times the station has been extended and modernised to cater for the annual influx of tourists, with train movements controlled by colour-light signals, although everything has been done tastefully and in keeping with this picturesque location.

On then to the final ¾ mile of our journey, opened to passengers on 22 May 1976, *Sir Haydn's* exhaust echoing round the valley as we wound our way above Abergynolwyn village. All too soon but right on time at 10.54 we entered Nant Gwernol, at which point the TR formerly collected the Bryn Eglwys slate from the foot of a gravity worked incline.

Time can be profitably spent exploring the beautiful area around Nant Gwernol, but on this occasion I returned to Tywyn with *Sir Haydn* which required little attention on the mainly downhill run. Travelling cab-first I had an unimpeded view ahead and could best appreciate the vast amount of work done on the railway over the past 30 years, it being hard to visualise the ramshackle state that greeted those preservation pioneers back in 1950.

Arrival at Tywyn meant for me the end of a never to be forgotten journey, but for the crew there was barely half-an-hour to snatch a bite to eat and prepare *Sir Haydn* for another trip — for him just part of the daily routine. The spirit of Sir Haydn does indeed live on at Tywyn.

ywyn to Nant Gwernol . . .
   Greasing *Sir Haydn's* motion.
   Tending the fire.
   Tywyn Wharf — the road ahead.
   Refreshment at Dolgoch Falls.

5 Token exchange at Abergynolwyn.
6 Waiting to leave Abergynolwyn.
7 Nant Gwernol — journey's end.

(G T Heavyside)

Strong and healthy at 114 years of age! Talyllyn
Railway 0-4-2ST No 1 *Talyllyn,* which was delivered
new to the line from Fletcher Jennings of Whitehaven in
1865, sturdily climbs the Afon Fathew valley between
Quarry Sidings and Abergynolwyn on 31 May 1979.
Unusually for narrow gauge lines TR stock has side buf-
fers and link couplings instead of the more usual centre
buffer/coupler. *(G T Heavyside)*

On the same day Andrew Barclay 0-4-0WT No 6
Douglas leaves Dolgoch Falls with the 15.25 Tywyn
Nant Gwernol. *(G T Heavyside)*

n 16 September 1978 *Talyllyn* eases its train across
the graceful Dolgoch viaduct — a view that in recent
years has become as familiar as many popular locations
in the main lines.   *(G T Heavyside)*

With the day's work over and the shadows lengthening
Douglas poses outside Tywyn Pendre engine shed
before retiring for the night on 31 May 1979. *Talyllyn* is
also visible in the left background.   *(G T Heavyside)*

Above: The tranquillity of the woods is shattered as 0-4-2ST No 3 *Sir Haydn* pulls away from Abergynolwyn with the 12.30 from Tywyn on the last stage of its journey to Nant Gwernol on 14 September 1978.

(G T Heavyside)

Top right: Modern steam technology comes to th narrow gauge! In 1958 Talyllyn Railway 0-4-2ST No *Edward Thomas* (Kerr Stuart No 4047 built 192 became the first British engine to be fitted with a Gie ejector, the brainchild of Austrian inventor Dr Adol Giesl-Gieslingen to improve draughting and boiler ef ciency, and while it found favour with many countri overseas only two were subsequently tried on B although the NCB purchased 46 sets. The distincti oblong ejector, an integral part of the Giesl, is promine in this view of *Edward Thomas* at work on 17 Augu 1968.

(G W Morriso

Right: Now running again with a more convention chimney following removal of the Giesl, *Edwa Thomas* takes a brief respite at Abergynolwyn durin journey to Nant Gwernol on 31 May 1979.

(G T Heavysid

The 11¾ mile 1ft 11½in gauge Vale of Rheidol Railway from Aberystwyth to Devil's Bridge is the only narrow gauge line now owned by British Rail, and since August 1968, when the last remaining standard gauge steam locomotives were withdrawn from service, its only line operated entirely by steam traction. All traffic is in the hands of three 2-6-2Ts, two built by the GWR in 1923, while No 9 *Prince of Wales* is a 1924 rebuild of one of the original engines supplied for the opening of the line in 1902 by Davies & Metcalfe of Romiley, Stockport. The engines sport blue livery and the BR double arrow emblem, but in deference to their GWR lineage the chimneys are copper capped.

Left: No 9 *Prince of Wales* pounds up the last few yards to Aberffrwd with the 10.15 from Aberystwyth on 1 June 1979. *(G T Heavyside)*

Right: Later the same day *Prince of Wales* takes a well-earned rest at Devil's Bridge before returning to the coast. *(G T Heavyside)*

Below: As part of BR, the Vale of Rheidol line is able to call on the expertise of British Rail Engineering Ltd for overhaul and repair and in May 1976 No 7 *Owain Glyndŵr* is seen inside Swindon Works waiting to be reunited with its boiler. *(J A M Vaughan)*

Above: Since 1968, when Vale of Rheidol trains first used the main Aberystwyth station, utilising the closed Carmarthen line platforms, the former standard gauge engine shed has housed the Rheidol stock. On 1 June 1979 *Prince of Wales* stands outside the shed, while on the left can be seen the main line to Shrewsbury. Notice the new position of the number plate high on the cabside displaced by the raised arrow symbol on the lower part of the cab. *(G T Heavyside)*

Below: No 8 *Llywelyn* rattles across the wooden bridge spanning the Afon Rheidol at Llanbadarn with an afternoon train from Aberystwyth on 15 September 1978. *(G T Heavyside)*

Right upper: In its first season as an oil fired engine Llywelyn nears the end of the continuous four mile 1 i 50 climb from Aberffrwd to Devil's Bridge with th 13.30 from Aberystwyth on 1 June 1979. *(G T Heavyside*

Right: No 7 *Owain Glyndŵr* has his thirst quenched a Devil's Bridge in July 1969. During the winter c 1977-8 the engine was converted to oil firing. *(L A Nixor*

Isle of Man

On a clear day from the top of Snaefell, the highest mountain on the Isle of Man, parts of England, Scotland, Wales and Northern Ireland can be seen, yet this 227 square mile island, while a crown possession, forms no part of the United Kingdom, and retains its own form of self government. In keeping, the Island's steam railway, in common with other things, perpetuates its own individuality and charm.

Perhaps surprisingly the railway age did not reach the Island until July 1873 when the Isle of Man Railway 3ft gauge Douglas to Peel route opened, followed by the Port Erin line in August 1874, although it was left to another company, the Manx Northern, to link Ramsey to the system in 1879. Construction of the 2½ mile Foxdale branch seven years later, built primarily to serve some local lead mines, completed the basic network that formed the backbone of the Island's transport needs for many decades.

Under a 1904 Act of Tynwald (the Manx Parliament) the IOMR took over the other lines and, apart from abandoning the Foxdale branch in 1941, continued unscathed for another 60 years. However the 1950s and 1960s were times of declining fortunes, with many services cut to effect economies, including complete winter closure of some lines (a far cry from 1920 when over 1½ million passengers were carried). In November 1965, with maintenance at a low ebb and only five of the 16 locomotives operable, all services were withdrawn for the winter. Later the subsequent announcement, that no trains would run in 1966, was greeted with little surprise.

At first Manx steam seemed to have died without ceremony, but from April 1967 the railway was leased for 21 years to a group headed by the Marquis of Ailsa, although the laudable intention of running trains throughout the Island proved too ambitious and faltered after two years. With financial assistance from the Manx Government the group then confined operations to the Port Erin route for another three years before exercising an option to ter-

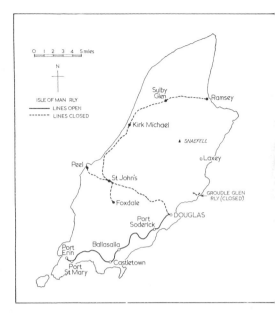

minate their tenure. Control then reverted t the IOMR which operated various sections o the southern limb (with grant aid) until Autum 1977 when Tynwald purchased the assets, thu nationalising the railway.

Throughout, traffic has mainly been handle by a fleet of 15 2-4-0Ts built by Beyer Peacoc between 1873 and 1926 with only detail di ferences, and 13 are still intact. The lines hav hosted three other steam engines, all supplied t the MNR, these being two 1879-built Shar Stewart 2-4-0Ts (both scrapped by 1923) an 0-6-0T *Caledonia* from Dübs in 1885. The latte is now enshrined in Port Erin Railwa Museum, opened in 1975, along with the fir and ultimate Beyer Peacock engines, Nos *Sutherland* and 16 *Mannin*. Steam's monopol has only been challenged by two diesel railca purchased from the County Donegal Railway i 1961.

With a forward looking policy unde nationalisation the future looks quite brig and hopefully trains will continue to shutt between Douglas and Port Erin indefinitely, f it would be a sad day should this route, like i northern counterparts and the Island's oth steam railway, the 2ft gauge Groudle Gl Railway which last ran in 1962, ever fade in total oblivion.

A reminder of a bygone era. Beyer Peacock 2-4-0T No
2 *Hutchinson,* in sight of the Irish Sea between St
John's and Kirk Michael heads for Ramsey with the
10.20 from Douglas on 21 June 1968, during the last
year trains ran on the Peel and Ramsey lines.   *(G D King)*

The distinctive lines of the Beyer Peacock 2-4-0Ts, with
their polished brass domes and tall chimneys bearing the
engine's numeral, are seen in this view of No 4 *Loch*
outside Port Erin shed on 23 August 1971. Engines of
this class have handled all the traffic in recent years.

(G T Heavyside)

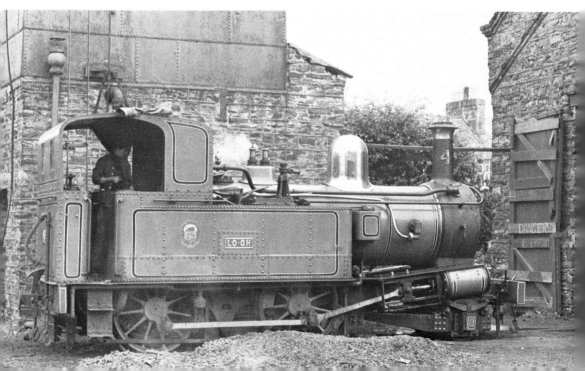

Above: On occasions, out of service engines have been exhibited at Douglas, and on 1 July 1971 No 13 *Kissack* returns no less than eight to the carriage sheds towards the end of the working day. Behind *Kissack* are Nos 9 *Douglas,* 1 *Sutherland,* 3 *Pender,* 14 *Thornhill,* 8 *Fenella,* 15 *Caledonia,* (the only 0-6-0T to work on the IOMR), 6 *Peveril* and 16 *Mannin.*   (*G D King*)

Right: Kissack makes a spirited departure from the imposing terminal station at Douglas, the Island's capital, with the 14.15 to Port Erin on 19 August 1971. The platform canopies have since been removed.

(*G T Heavyside*)

No 4 *Loch,* built in 1874, waits impatiently for departure time at Port Erin on 21 August 1971 with the 10.15 for Douglas. *(G T Heavyside)*

Afternoon crossing at Ballasalla as No 11 *Maitland* leaves for Port Erin, while on the left another train returns to Douglas, on 24 August 1971.
(G T Heavyside)

Sunlight and shade at Castletown, the Manx capital until 1869, as No 12 *Hutchinson* heads west for Port Erin on 20 August 1971.　　　　　*(G T Heavyside)*

No 13 *Kissack* attacks Nunnery Bank, on the outskirts of Douglas, with the 10.15 Douglas-Port Erin on 29 May 1972.　　　　　*(L A Nixon)*

Ireland

Ireland's railways have differed in various ways from those on the mainland, for the principal routes were constructed to a gauge of 5ft 3in, while in the latter part of the nineteenth century numerous secondary lines of 3ft gauge sprang up. Mainly these served rural and sparsely populated areas, and in many instances provided feeder services for the main lines, akin to some overseas practice.

The first 3ft gauge line authorised by Parliament, was the 16 mile Ballymena, Cushendall & Red Bay Railway, opened in 1875, following which track was laid apace until lines totalling 530 miles, owned by 19 separate concerns, were fragmented throughout Ireland. Many owed their existence to the Tramways Act of 1883 and subsequent Acts of Parliament, whereby financial assistance and various guarantees were given by the government and local authorities to companies providing a railway where this was considered desirable. Steam was generally the norm but two lines, the Giants Causeway and the Bessbrook & Newry, used electric traction, while the nine mile Listowel & Ballybunion Railway lays claim to fame as Britain's only Lartigue monorail line, which regrettably operated for no more than 36 years from 1888.

However from the 1920s the 3ft gauge gradually declined in importance as the ravages of politics and harsh economics, both north and south of the border, took its toll; the last steam line of all, the Cavan & Leitrim Railway, concluded business in April 1959. Even the use of diesel railcars from the 1930s on what was the most extensive system, the County Donegal Joint lines, and complete dieselisation during the early 1950s of the West Clare line did not ensure their future, the latter being the last to close in February 1961.

While as a public carrier 3ft wide track is obsolete, the gauge is still used extensively by the Bord Na Mona (Irish Turf Board) and by other industrial concerns, but alas all use internal combustion engines, as do the remaining smaller gauge lines.

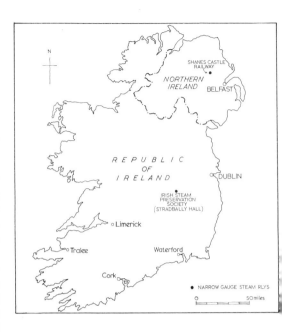

One former system worthy of note was the 1ft 10in gauge complex operated until 1975 at the Dublin brewery of Arthur Guinness Son & Co (Dublin) Ltd, where track on two levels was connected by a narrow spiral tunnel. After earlier engines had not proved entirely satisfactory, the company engineer Samuel Geoghegan designed a diminutive locomotive with the cylinders set above the boiler, the drive transmitted by vertical rods. The prototype was built by Avonside in 1882, followed by a further 18 from William Spence of Dublin — the only engines built by this firm. These unique engines could also work the company's 5ft 3in gauge track by utilising a cradle wagon.

Fortunately examples from the golden days of narrow gauge steam have been preserved at various locations, and in recent years steam has returned to the 3ft gauge on new lines at Shane's Castle in Northern Ireland, and at Stradbally Hall in the Republic, and these form suitable memorials, both live and static, to an age when the iron horse was part of the everyday scene along the country byways of the Emerald Isle.

The pastoral nature of Ireland's 3ft gauge systems is captured by this view of Tralee & Dingle Railway Hunslet-built 2-6-0Ts Nos 1T and 2T running into Annascaul with an empty cattle train bound for Dingle on 29 June 1951. This train, then the only service operating on the line, was run monthly in connection with Dingle fair until June 1953, when the line closed.
(Ivo Peters)

Former Bord Na Mona Andrew Barclay 0-4-0WT No 2 (works No 2264 of 1949) in action on the Irish Steam Preservation Society's 3ft gauge track at Stradbally Hall, Stradbally, Co Laois. *(S J Carse)*

Above: Standing resplendent in the Guinness Museum, at the St James's Gate Brewery of Arthur Guinness Son & Co (Dublin) Ltd, Dublin, is one of the unique 1ft 10in gauge Spence 0-4-0Ts built for the brewery system, this being No 17 of 1902. In all seven of these engines have been preserved, five in Ireland and two in Britain.
(Courtesy Guinness Museum)

Right upper: Positively glowing in the afternoon sunshine during June 1976 is Peckett 0-4-0T No 1 *Tyrone* on the 1½ mile, 3ft gauge Shane's Castle Railway, near Antrim, opened in 1971, on the northern banks of Lough Neagh, the largest expanse of fresh water in the British Isles. *Tyrone,* constructed in 1904, was originally employed by the British Aluminium Co at Larne harbour.
(C P Friel,

Right: The following month *Tyrone* barks up Millburn bank with a full compliment of passengers. In conjunction with the Royal Society for the Protection of Birds a nature reserve has also been established at Shane's Castle, the residence of the House of O'Neill for centuries.
(Courtesy Lord O'Neill

Narrow Gauge Septet

The grace, charm, richness, and variety of the narrow gauge steam scene is illustrated by this montage of photographs . . .

1 Talyllyn Railway 0-4-2ST *Edward Thomas*.
2 Ravenglass & Eskdale Railway 2-8-2 *River Esk*.
3 Festiniog Railway 2-4-0ST plus tender *Blanche*.

4 Romney, Hythe & Dymchurch Railway 4-6-2 *Southern Maid*.
5 Leighton Buzzard Narrow Gauge Railway 0-4-0S *Pixie*.
6 Snowdon Mountain Railway 0-4-2T *Eryri*.
7 Isle of Man Railway 2-4-0T *Maitland*.

. . . long may their like continue to delight u
(G T Heavysid